SAD LITTLE BREATHING MACHINE

SAD LITTLE BREATHING MACHINE

POEMS BY

MATTHEA HARVEY

Graywolf Press
Saint Paul, Minnesota

Publication of this volume is made possible in part by a grant provided by the Minnesota State Arts Board, through an appropriation by the Minnesota State Legislature; a grant from the Wells Fargo Foundation Minnesota; and a grant from the National Endowment for the Arts. Significant support has also been provided by the Bush Foundation; Target, Marshall Field's and Mervyn's with support from the Target Foundation; the McKnight Foundation; and other generous contributions from foundations, corporations, and individuals. To these organizations and individuals we offer our heartfelt thanks.

Special funding for this title has been provided by the Jerome Foundation.

MINNESOTA
STATE ARTS BOARD

NATIONAL
ENDOWMENT
FOR THE ARTS

TARGET.

Published by Graywolf Press
2402 University Avenue, Suite 203
Saint Paul, Minnesota 55114
All rights reserved.

www.graywolfpress.org

Published in the United States of America

ISBN-10: 1-55597-396-5
ISBN-13: 978-1-55597-396-4

2   4   6   8   9   7   5   3

Library of Congress Control Number: 2003111079

Cover design: Jeenee Lee

Cover art: Rebecca Horn, *The Unconsciousness of Feelings*
Represented by Holzwarth Publications

FOR R.

CONTENTS

3   Introduction to the World

4   Bird Transfer

5   Life-Size Is What We Are (A New History of Photography)

6   To Zanzibar by Motorcar

7   Baked Alaska, a Theory Of

8   No More Frisson Please

9   Toe the Line with Me

10 If You Like Sugar I'll Like Sugar Too

11 Save the Originals

12 Sad Little Breathing Machine

15 Introduction to Eden

16 Equation with Flowers

17 Poem Including the Seven Deadly Sins

18 The Crowds Cheered As Gloom Galloped Away

19 Trouble in the Dyad

20 This Is Not a Glass Door

21 Our Square of Lawn

23 First Person Fabulous

24 Shiver & You Have Weather

27 Introduction to Circumference

28 Poem Including the Seven Wonders of the Ancient World

29 Diagram of Pretty Please

30 O the Zoetrope & the Periscope Should Be Friends

31 Sergio Valente, Sergio Valente,
     How You Look Tells the World How You Feel

32 Ideas Go Only So Far

33 Not So Much Miniature As Far Away
34 The Unconsciousness of Feelings
35 Snowglobe Hypothesis

39 Introduction to Addiction
40 Introduction to a Diction
41 Grand Narrative with Chandelier
42 Machine for Jean Rhys
43 Introduction to the Swanhouse
44 You're Miss Reading
45 Definition of Weather
46 The Crying Fields
47 Address to an Absent Flea

51 Introduction to Narrative
52 Once upon a Time: A Genre Fable
54 Meat Ravioli vs. Spaghetti Bolognese
55 Sentenced: The Subject Objects to Its Long-
    Distance Relationship with the Object
56 Reverberations in the Snail / World
57 Color by Number
58 The Difference Between the Need for Consistency
    & the State of Expectation
60 The Transparent Heir Apparent
61 Can We See

65 Introduction to the End
66 Introduction to Disease

67   That Was the First Day & We Never Forgot It

68   Town of Then

69   A Ruffle, a Rendezvous

70   Abandoned Conversation with the Senses

71   Reverse Space Invaders

72   Limelight Memorandum

73   Going Off the Deep End into Confectionery

74   Everything Must Go

INTRODUCTION TO THE WORLD

For the time being
call me Home.

All the ingenues do.

Units are the engines
I understand best.

One betrayal, two.
Merrily, merrily, merrily.

Define hope.   Machine.
Define machine.   Nope.

Like thoughts,
the geniuses race through.

If you're lucky

after a number of
revolutions, you'll

feel something catch.

BIRD TRANSFER

Unfasten the crows & the clouds
come crashing down. It's a window

into the lightning-struck-ago:
diamond sunspots on the videotape,

coins hitting the fountain floor.
Invent the sun & edition the trees.

Center your swan on the pond.

LIFE-SIZE IS WHAT WE ARE
(A NEW HISTORY OF PHOTOGRAPHY)

Selflessly the self gave it all away.
Pin all yr hopes, lay all yr love, etc.

Which means the fish that live
in a plastic bag think the edges

of the world pucker. It's one thing to
make an image. It's two things to find one.

Why weren't we mindful of the lady
behind the makeup counter, calling,

"Come here honey, let me give you
some eyes"? The laws were sunsetting.

One puff of smoke rose in the minefield.
People dragged their shadows along.

I'm here to tell you that you're not.
Surprise, darling, surprise.

TO ZANZIBAR BY MOTORCAR

In Regensberg, the cloud
left the mountain. In vain

I crumpled my crinolines,
scuffed the sand outside the temple.

My eyes took in only eye-shaped
things—mouseface flickering

in the mousehole, pansies
twitching with palsy. Where

the squint & the kiss are common,
there are no rebels lurking

between the 15th & 16th parallel.
Children are symmetrical

& zebras fingerprint the plains.
Ask me if I'm pretending

& I will freeze to delineate
my non-nod from my nod.

BAKED ALASKA, A THEORY OF

The moat simmers at 210°. From his tower the king watches, pleased, as a swallow tries to land on the water, squawks & flies off. He believes in setting a good example. *O the flesh is hot but the heart is cold, you'll be alone when you are old,* his favorite country song— on repeat—is being piped through the palace. Downstairs in the dining room, the princesses gaze out the window at a flock of pigeons turning pink then black as they fly in & out of the sunset. The princesses put down their spoons & sigh. Baked Alaska for dessert again. The flambé lights up their downcast faces. When dinner is over, they return to their wing of the palace, The Right Ventricle. On a good day, they can play Hearts for a few hours before they hear the king's dactylic footsteps (*dámn the queen, dámn the queen*) coming down the aorta & have to hide the cards. They aren't allowed to adore him, so they don't, just allow his inspections—checking their eyes for stars, their journals for heated confessions. Because he is a literal man, he never finds anything. But that night, when he's gone, the princesses tiptoe down to the palace freezer. Sticking their fingers in sockets is no longer enough. Amongst the frozen slabs of beef, they sit in a circle on blocks of ice & watch the red fade from their lips & fingers, the frost on the floor creep up the heels of their shoes. Finally when the skin is numb, the heat starts retreating into their hearts & they can feel it—love, love, love.

NO MORE FRISSON PLEASE

Engine: I must look nice
—> <— !

Irrelevant, irrelevant sang
the xylophone to the mallet,

though without it plinking
were impossible. The ether

wasn't working either.
We could still see budgies.

The whole house waited
while you twirled a tiny divan

between your fingers.
Ever tempted to linger, I

pixilated you, ate sugar
in the form of quince.

Haven't heard from you
since, hottie.

TOE THE LINE WITH ME

We needed water & frozen water
for the party. I chose you to two-step

with but the downstairs chandelier
stayed still, its prisms prim.

Consider this: if sunfish
& ducks compete for the same bit

of bread, at any moment their mouths
might meet. That's how my mother

explained the Other, told me to hedge
my bets, furl wish-scrolls into

the topiary. Still I had questions
about Life & the Afterlife. You

looked in through the screen door.
I sat next to my ex.

IF YOU LIKE SUGAR I'LL LIKE SUGAR TOO

I'm making a little machine.
Not everywhere do cows move

slowly among the trees like ideas.
Not everyone gets a dollop

of cream & some ground glass
to look through. It's a spectacle

all right. Help me attach the prism
to the jump rope. I sold the chapel

because it contained no nouns—
it wasn't even that I didn't

know the language. O you
& your faux-beurre sandwiches—

that otherworldly swallowing.
Please don't put your head

in the hay. Meet me at the beach
& we'll watch conditional holding hands

with conditional making an iffy
path through the sand.

SAVE THE ORIGINALS

For the entrance exam we have to match TV static to a daisy field. After years of practice (books & rocks, near & far), it's a breeze. At orientation, those with fluctuating weight or braces are pulled aside. Not ready. We, who will eventually copy, have chosen one hairstyle & smile & stuck to it —we have the class photos to prove it. Still, we're not allowed near the machines for weeks. The equals sign on the blackboard grows four-boxes-of-chalk thick. Pale sandwiches pile up in our lockers. Then one day we're told to take a left at the water fountain instead of a right, & we're in the copy room. I don't fiddle with the dials; I make a copy. I like him immediately. He looks like me but with darker circles under his my-eyes, a more pronounced scar on his my-cheek. When I look up, I see that Sylvia has made herself three copies at 10%, 35% & 75%. A Sylvia crescendo. I feel a hand on my back & then I don't look at anyone else anymore. For the first few nights, we stay up late. We are each other's perfect hug. He's thoughtful & helpful, my shadow with a shuffle—he plumps the sofa cushions, feeds the goldfish. I can tell from the way he studies Splash & Splish that he thinks Splash is the original & Splish is the copy. "How sweet," I think. One day, via the hallway mirror, I watch as he transfers Splash into a jam jar, then lets a golden handful of fish flakes fall gently into the bowl holding Splish. I'm at a distance but I know which is which. The next night my red scarf is missing from the front hall & so is he. My phone rings. The soprano has the flu & the understudy is performing. He's at the opera. We all are.

SAD LITTLE BREATHING MACHINE

Engine: @

Under its glass lid, the square
of cheese is like any other element

of the imagination—cough in the tugboat,
muff summering somewhere in mothballs.

Have a humbug. The world is slow
to dissolve & leave us. Is it your

hermeneut's helmet not letting me
filter through? The submarine sinks

with a purpose: Scientist Inside
Engineering A Shell. & meanwhile

I am not well. Don't know how to go on
Oprah without ya. On TV, a documentary

about bees—yet another box in a box.
The present is in there somewhere.

INTRODUCTION TO EDEN

Call me What You Will.

This for your complicated hands—
my best mechanical tree.

Test?	No thank you.
Question?	The rivers run in circles.
You noticed.	We noticed.

(thinking)

Duet!	& the pin factory . . .

Sweet extrovert, it is making pins.

You will, you know,	
but I shouldn't sing	Introvert! Introvert!
if I were you	

in case the gate sings back.

EQUATION WITH FLOWERS

The meringues were already
cloud-palaces, we didn't need

the greasy telescope to mother-
of-pearl the sky. When the sun sets,

the truck sometimes strays from
its appointed route with only

willows watching & perhaps
a horse. Clip-clop—where's the narrative?

Somewhere a frugivore is sitting on
its perch with juice matting its chin.

I can't write haughty essays or join
Scotland Yard in its never-ending

search for some one-syllable gem
while there are still apples in the world.

Do you remember that itch.
Even a fraction of it.

POEM INCLUDING THE SEVEN DEADLY SINS

William moved over & through
his submarine sandwich.

It was astonishing.
Everyone was astonished.

A mother's disapproving "tut" hung
between the affianced pair like a sloth

& *Everybody Shimmies Now*
played softly on the radio.

The new transparent shopping bags
concealed nothing & pilot lights

in stoves all over the city burned
tiny & true. If you couldn't covet

a privet hedge what could you covet.
The psychiatrist breathed onto the mirror

then licked his breath back off.
It was a dangerous time.

Tomorrow they would try to name
the luminous horse in the photograph.

THE CROWDS CHEERED AS GLOOM GALLOPED AWAY

Everyone was happier. But where did the sadness go? People wanted to know. They didn't want it collecting in their elbows or knees then popping up later. The girl who thought of the ponies made a lot of money. Now a month's supply of pills came in a hard blue case with a handle. You opened it & found the usual vial plus six tiny ponies of assorted shapes & sizes, softly breathing in the Styrofoam. Often they had to be pried out & would wobble a little when first put on the ground. In the beginning the children tried to play with them, but the sharp hooves nicked their fingers & the ponies refused to jump over pencil hurdles. The children stopped feeding them sugarwater & the ponies were left to break their legs on the gardens' gravel paths or drown in the gutters. On the first day of the month, rats gathered on doorsteps & spat out only the bitter manes. Many a pony's last sight was a bounding squirrel with its tail hovering over its head like a halo. Behind the movie theatre the hardier ponies gathered in packs amongst the cigarette butts, getting their hooves stuck in wads of gum. They lined the hills at funerals, huddled under folding chairs at weddings. It became a matter of pride if one of your ponies proved unusually sturdy. People would smile & say, "This would have been an awful month for me," pointing to the glossy palomino trotting energetically around their ankles. Eventually, the ponies were no longer needed. People had learned to imagine their sadness trotting away. & when they wanted something more tangible, they could always go to the racetrack & study the larger horses' faces. Gloom, #341, with those big black eyes, was almost sure to win.

TROUBLE IN THE DYAD

Though Ed said "You have my word
on it" as Diana ate her Ritz cracker,

there was something in the way
he said it. The shears choked on

the bonsai. Little maple, give us this—
one day without a weeping bout.

"Think!" he thought, irritated by
her ex-pensive ways. She had forgotten

that eventually skis get attached
to something unruly, like a person.

There they were, just going along
until Di started singing "Won't you

be my one & lonely?" which is
of course when he spotted the pyramid.

THIS IS NOT A GLASS DOOR

The fax went through
& through. In a way,

Fred meant to bump noses
with Mary. The protestors

fell asleep against
the fluffy barricade.

Quietly, lower
Paleolithic blended

with middle Paleolithic.
There was a tax on English

biscuits again.
A sign told you

when you were
in the park.

OUR SQUARE OF LAWN

From the parrot's perch
the view is always Hello.

We try not to greet one
another. When the boys come

after school I shout
"You are not cameras"

at them & they run away.
Fact will muzzle anything.

I look at myself in
a spoon & I am just

a head. Never learned
how to make ringlets—

was always too literal.
The trees are covered

with tiny dead bouquets.
The ducks have been eating

grass with chemicals on it,
ignoring the signs. At night

from our glass-fronted box
we watch them glow.

It is the closest we come
to dreaming.

FIRST PERSON FABULOUS

First Person fumed & fizzed under Third Person's tongue while Third Person slumped at the diner counter, talking, as usual, to no one. Third Person thought First Person was the toilet paper trailing from Third Person's shoe, the tiara Third Person once wore in a dream to a funeral. First Person thought Third Person was a layer of tar on a gorgeous pink nautilus, a foot on a fountain, a tin hiding the macaroons & First Person was that nautilus, that fountain, that pile of macaroons. Sometimes First Person broke free on first dates (with a Second Person) & then there was the delicious rush of "I this" and "I that" but then no phone call & for weeks Third Person wouldn't let First Person near anyone. Poor First Person. Currently she was exiled to the world of postcards *(having a lovely time)*—& even then that beast of a Third Person used the implied "I" just to drive First Person crazy. She felt like a television staring at the remote, begging to be turned on. She had so many things she wanted to say. If only she could survive on her own, she'd make Third Person choke on herself & when the detectives arrived & all eyes were on her, she'd cry out, "I did it! I did it! Yes, dahlings, it was me!"

SHIVER & YOU HAVE WEATHER

Engine: ☑ ☐

In the aftermath of calculus
your toast fell butter-side down.

Squirrels swarmed the lawns
in flight patterns. The hovercraft

helped the waves along. From
every corner there was perspective.

On the billboards the diamonds
were real, in the stores, only zirconia.

I cc'ed you. I let you know.
Sat down to write the Black Ice Memo.

Dinner would be meager &
reminiscent of next week's lunch.

So what if I sat on the sectional?
As always I was beside myself.

INTRODUCTION TO CIRCUMFERENCE

	Holding veined circles against the rain?
Definitive.	
	Iffy if you ask me.
& the little orange pills	
	—we like so much.
There you are.	Indeed.
Come now, you have furs & sugarplums.	One to a packet.
	Oh Sir, let us take a different walk.
	(gloom looping their ankles)
	Primarily we object to your making us hug.
Well I don't like fractions.	

POEM INCLUDING THE SEVEN WONDERS OF THE ANCIENT WORLD

The hologram hostas swung softly
in their macramé swing. If only

Alice would stop hitting her head
on the ceiling, but a body

Will Up. It was like croquet, really,
the way some ideas went through:

love triangle instead of lust-
isosceles, Mama flashing a mirror

so we'd find our way home.
Another tick of the kaleidoscope

& a little girl is hunting
marbles beneath the trees &

Chairman Mao, so lean & mistrustful,
is studying the plans for his heli-car.

The thing is, of course, how to land.

DIAGRAM OF PRETTY PLEASE

On skis, I crisscross the plaza—
doorstep to stoplight, think to thought.

Let the thistle leave the forest discreetly
on the possum. Let the sweet buns

in the bakery window overlap
& smudge their icing. Inasmuch

as my arms are full of compass roses,
I know exactly where I'm going.

That's my love there in the swivel chair.
I'm the sugarbowl on wheels.

O THE ZOETROPE & THE PERISCOPE SHOULD BE FRIENDS

We sequestered the slices of lemon
to better understand the bitterness.
The pretty city shifted.

Girls who could see around
corners whispered "or"
to one another. Their handkerchiefs

were as one handkerchief
floating across a field
home to a critical white horse.

The truce translated thusly:
a pennant by every pond.
Each chose their favorite view:

they were all things
we had invented.
We called the cat perturbed.

SERGIO VALENTE, SERGIO VALENTE, HOW YOU LOOK TELLS THE WORLD HOW YOU FEEL

Engine: $< : \emptyset : \square$

My "you" came to the city to visit
me: clouds rushed between us

& the sun. The albums were finally full.
Halfheartedly we looked through lenses,

fish-eye & wide, but we'd had enough
likenesses taken. Similes were simply out

of the question. The blind man, regardless,
said, "Please a little light so I can see

my love." (He'd gone through
seven doves without knowing it.) In bed,

the surveyors held their aching heads.
Satellites caught our thoughts & held them.

Then snow fell in between two trains;
then fleas swirled in the hoof-dust; & when

we looked at each other we didn't look
alike. I kissed your magnifying glass

& said, "When the aliens come,
they'll know we're inside our cars."

IDEAS GO ONLY SO FAR

Last year I made up a baby. I made her in the shape of a hatbox or a cake. I could have iced her & no one would have been the wiser. You know how trained elephants will step onto a little round platform, cramming all four fat feet together? That's her too, & the fez on the elephant's head. Applause all around. There was no denying I had made a good baby. I gave her a sweet face, a pair of pretty eyes, & a secret trait at her christening. I set her on my desk, face up, & waited. I watched her like a clock. I didn't coo at her though. She wasn't that kind of baby.

She never got any bigger, but she did learn to roll. Her little flat face went round & round. On her other side, her not-face rolled round & round too. She followed me everywhere. When I swam, she floated in the swimming pool, a platter for the sun. When I read, she was my peacefully blinking footstool. She fit so perfectly into the washing machine that perhaps I washed her more than necessary. But it was wonderful to watch her eyes slitted against the suds, a stray red sock swishing about her face like the tongue of some large animal.

When you make up a good baby, other people will want one too. Who's to say that I'm the only one who deserves a dear little machine-washable ever-so-presentable baby. Not me. So I made a batch. But they weren't exactly like her—they were smaller & without any inborn dread. Sometimes I see one rolling past my window at sunset—quite unlike my baby, who like any good idea, eventually ended up dead.

NOT SO MUCH MINIATURE AS FAR AWAY

Little was left of the forest.
Large was ten miles ahead.

The song on the radio
was early 80s in a nutshell,

the sun in the rearview
mirror, a peach pit of light.

Make much of me why don't you.
All sorts land at the airfield.

Be silverfish, be blimp.

THE UNCONSCIOUSNESS OF FEELINGS

Praying mantises patrolled the peepholes,
tilting their triangular heads. The lookout

rode the Ferris wheel—ground / tree / bird /
sky / bird / tree / ground—& in the confusion

caused by a sudden profusion of posies,
the train tracks slid through.

Lo, the electrical boxes stopped
clicking as we walked past. The richest man

in the world traded his yell for a smile.
Someone in a red shirt began to run

behind the trees each night in a poor imitation
of sunset. She was thrilled & unwell.

I suppose I can say it—she was me.
I missed the mother bird who dropped

her babies on my glass ceiling, missed
their tiny pterodactyl shadows on my floor.

They were so beautiful projected there.

SNOWGLOBE HYPOTHESIS

By way of the elevator the smell
traveled from floor to floor—

Argument For, as in the new blender
snug in its casement of foam,

or the stewardess on her roof garden,
breeding those mini-suns,

chrysanthemums, for the light-starved
below. These & other thoughts rattled

around the astronaut's helmeted head.
His breath fogged the moonscape.

Aladdin, poor lad, wanted out,
not in. We closed our eyes & still

we could see him, which meant
Argument Against, which meant

if oilspill, if imperfect pancake, then
tupperware, terrarium, gumball machine.

INTRODUCTION TO ADDICTION

Sirs, do you know me?

Sugar, we get up because you do.

& you like the hologram daisies?

Off & on, yes.

Don't get all and/or on me
like Red Riding, that little hoodlum,
"saving all her cakes for grandma."

Victim may turn blue.

You know I made you

that clever
& you're here for us if we'll

just come in

to a bit of money.

The bottles are beautiful, though.

Beautiful. God. Yes.

INTRODUCTION TO A DICTION

Galoshless, I
stood by the river, all ashiver.   Gosh I was hoping for liver.

That's enough Charlie Parker.

Open your dictionaries please.   Open your dictionaries please.

Bravo: the cattleguard caught nary a hoof!

                                        The poet is certain
                                        rain makes the moat brim.

I am crestfallen.   Understood (Flatterer).

Now was I going to wade in?   Not without the correct equipment.
& the shipment arrives . . .   Wednesday, Wednesday, from across the sea.

GRAND NARRATIVE WITH CHANDELIER

People woke to find watches
in their hair. It meant

we were missing something.
It meant the pot of face-cream

could turn ominous on us.
No one cheered when the two

square twins were born,
though we'd all been waiting.

The gasoline rings in the puddles
were beautiful but unreadable.

We craved butter, were critical
of any play that lacked a love seat.

The lipstick gig was rescinded
when the winner's close-ups

revealed tiny robots helping
her ballgown float behind her

& when just the stems
of champagne glasses appeared

on the assembly line suddenly
we could see the end.

MACHINE FOR JEAN RHYS

It's all lit up with handfuls
& eyefuls & it doesn't want you

because that's what you want.
Flicker, the land shrugs off

its scape, flicker, the trees fall
away. If la lumière is stoppered

in bottles what is the light
over there? What in the world

do you want in the world?
If the café had stayed,

the waiter would know.
If those eyes were

your own, you might also.

INTRODUCTION TO THE SWANHOUSE

Call me Swanhaus.

Kissed yourselves good night
again last night?

Time to polish   Thought the world
the windows again.   was broader.

                                        But the bits of light.

oh dear / Scatterbrain.

It is a scatterbrain also.

                                        & now?

Innovator aren't you.

                                        Now.

Preen preen preen.

                                        What is that?

Izzat.

Drat. Outsonneted
meself again.

YOU'RE MISS READING

Engine: ≅

All bright thought lay in future thought.
The coin was in the puddin' hid.

Cod from the machine will not do,
said the dramaturg-turned-nutritionist.

Only the upper echelons could afford to be
nonchalant about it. They were, as in, oh.

It was the first time a lost Jocelyn
& a found Jocelyn had turned out

to be not one & the same.
The trial continued.

You're Miss Reading, aren't you?

                               Yes.

*& you still refuse to name
the cake in question?*

                               *Earlier in the hearing, I considered
relenting, but now that you put it
that way—yes.*

DEFINITION OF WEATHER

(abbr.)	W.
(accus.)	You little wretch.
(anat.)	Organs of indeterminate rumbling.
(attrib. false) Ashbery	My charming weather-wuss, I'll wed you in Anatolia.
(bibl.)	Elijah asked the brothers to stop throwing stones at their sister. They did not stop. The next day an asteroid killed their pet rabbit.
(cinetamog.)	*The Divan's Demise*—real-time footage of raindrops coming through the window & staining a lavender velvet sofa. (129 min.)
(colloq.) "under the weather"	Aren't we all.
(culin.)	Pancake ice.
(demons.)	Zeus, *this* is the unnecessary storm I was talking about.
(ellip.)	Ergo.
(exclam.)	Your oracular bones!
(fem.)	Hurricane Helen
(hist.)	Queen Victoria's coronation: raindrops break & enter into what had been ordained A Fine Day.
(mil.)	Cloud Formations
(ornithol.)	Initially canaries were thought to fall from the clouds after a tropical storm.
(poet.)	Reverse ascension.
(sl.) tornadoes & hurricanes	Cones 'n Canes
(theol.)	Yes.

THE CRYING FIELDS

Dew rose from the ground & no tears fell. Fireflies in the field beaconed, beckoned & if you ran toward them, shouting "A star, a star," inevitably you killed them & the light went out. It was an old trick & everyone knew it. Likewise the sick swans in the lake, the sentimental novels piled under the trees. Babies were born smiling despite the copious slapping that welcomed them to the world. Only The Town Crier, on his rustproof platform, wept & wept. His disciples caught his tears & smeared them on their faces, brought him pitchers of water to keep the tears coming. When it rained, the fakers ran around wailing "Alas, alas," as if they were fooling anyone. Under bright umbrellas, the non-believers (who nonetheless didn't want to go back to their happy homes) prowled the periphery, keeping their faces defiantly dry. Their leader had an idea. Tomorrow they'd kidnap the old S.O.B. & turn him into a fountain.

ADDRESS TO AN ABSENT FLEA

Reading the sonnet the old way
was impossible once the period

started leaping about. Through
the magnifying glass you seemed

a gadget God, with a suitably
parasitical air. I am trying not

to let making too much of things
become a habit—I read too slowly

already. Little Itch-Ticket whose
menu has only one item on it,

I think it's important to be specific.
I've never felt desire before.

I won't believe that was accidental
syntax. If a pen were a turret to me

I too might wait, nest in a tapestry
& save my stories for some bloodless day,

but please come back from wherever
you've gone. There is so little left.

INTRODUCTION TO NARRATIVE

Call me Content.

I don't need an introduction.   No.

For fun then—

Tick
                                        table of contents
Tock.

handholds in the cliff   they fall in love
snow fills the fireplace   fall out of love
water laps at the sand   reunited reunited

—pause as narrator snuffles around the edges of the icerink—

                    "Be nice be nice!"
                    cried the terrified populace.
                    Then wheedling: Beautiful scaffolding,
                    how I love you.

Soon you shall receive the commemorative spoon.

                    Then call me content too.

ONCE UPON A TIME: A GENRE FABLE

"That little Narrative is so adorable," said Neighbor Lady One to the baby's proud Mama & indeed she was, nestled there in her pram like a love scene in between pages of description. Papa called her his *bella novella,* lifted her over his head & cried, "subtext, subtext!" This was before the Terrible Twos & the Fictional Fours, before she was caught herding the neighbor children around an abandoned plot of land with a splintered 2x4. At first she had seemed quite normal. So what if she wailed when a pea she flung from her highchair was left on the floor, wailed until her action reached its logical conclusion—parent retrieves pea, pea is put in the trash. So what if she liked to arrange the pigeons on her window ledge. "She's so strong-willed," said the school psychologist, remembering her first encounter with the little girl who had angrily denied plagiarizing her 2nd grade book report entitled, "Tiny Tolstoy Dreamed of Postponing Bedtime by Making His Mama Read a Much Bigger Book."

For a while Narrative formed a trio with two malleable girls whom she happily ordered around, but then they turned thirteen & Poetry & Art began to behave unpredictably in the presence of boys. Annoyed, Narrative withdrew into television—mainly sitcoms & after a particularly explicit documentary about slaughterhouses, changed her beloved pony's name from First Pet to Glue. She hated high school. Being made to switch subjects after fifty minutes made her feel homicidal. So mostly she hung out in the park slowly smoking 100s & watching the flowers turn their heads from west to east. She didn't mind the shady characters who shuffled around. At least they knew what flashbacks were.

(Weeks passed.) Then one day her wristwatch stopped. The watchmaker's was shut so she strode up the hill to the watch factory which ticked &

tocked on a hill above town. Even as she turned the doorknob she sensed a plot twist coming on. There, before her, on thin silver legs, was the most beautiful structure she had ever seen: an assembly line with, bless it, a definite beginning, middle & end. It even came complete with a hero (the foreperson) & villain (a slow woman whose hands shook as she slipped the tiny gold second hand over the minute & hour hands, while watches piled up at her station). Narrative & the foreperson rolled their eyes simultaneously. He hired her on the spot & gave her the delightful job of welding the finished watches shut. Of course she fell for the foreperson. Of course theirs was a storybook romance—he too hated modern dance, loved layercake, knew just the setting she'd want for her wedding ring. In time they had a child whom they named Memoir, a baby girl who somehow seemed to be taking notes from the first moment her mouth clamped onto Narrative's nipple.

MEAT RAVIOLI VS. SPAGHETTI BOLOGNESE

Little girls sat on the edge of the pool
like bright-bellied newts. Their parents

were paler. For a quarter, the shoe-polishing
machine would polish one shoe, then the other.

Or it could do the same shoe twice so that
headlights would flicker across it

& not the other. The P.I. listlessly
dusted for fingerprints. He was saving

up for a TV & a lock. In Schenectady
the criminal pressed a scalloped hanky

to each cheek & wondered aloud,
mockingly, "O where might I be?"

Each film mentioned at the dinner party
was a sinkhole we skirted so as not to fall

into story. It's like Pete & Betty always said:
self as discrete package or self in the world.

SENTENCED: THE SUBJECT OBJECTS TO ITS LONG-DISTANCE RELATIONSHIP WITH THE OBJECT

Engine: <u>you |are</u> | <u>Who</u>

I awoke to a nest-scuffle between
Gosling One & Gosling Two.

The doorbell cored a pathway from
outside to in. Either or but not and.

Were you here, I'd say, "what if clouds
looked like planes before planes

looked like clouds" or tell you about
the town in Iceland where a snoet wrote

a snoem on the back of its favorite yak.
Fact is, you're my cake behind glass,

missed kerfuffle in the cloakroom.
Sleep is dreamier—there grasses graze

on sheep & the newspapers run
this headline:
        Boy Thinks "Girl." "Boy" Thinks Girl.

REVERBERATIONS IN THE SNAIL / WORLD

Engine: _@_

She went pedaling by—
Nystagmus (Sir Roving Eye)

addressed the before & after.
With his verb-foot he is always

making sentences. As subjects latch
onto objects, he found her—

whir of pedal-circles,
bicycle trail post-puddle.

West of this week: no kiss
on the cheek. To the east,

reverie, reverie.

COLOR BY NUMBER

At eight the gate clicks open.
The shrubs indent themselves   just so.

Behind us pebbles rise up
through the paths. Bird machines

trouble the foliage. A valve
hisses & the violets *bloom.*

Then according to plan, we hijack
a pram & trap a portable puddle.

It is anxious & looks like us.
We almost take it home.

Instead, we hide in the hedge
& wait to throw it. We've a mind

to change the weather.

THE DIFFERENCE BETWEEN THE NEED FOR CONSISTENCY
& THE STATE OF EXPECTATION

Engine: /_

The mouse moved like a sugar
mouse. The plank factory wasn't

without razzle-dazzle—Hazel,
the foreperson, had an upturned

nose. At one time snow
could be counted upon to

highlight the horizontal. We were
Learning to Love the Organism

at Large, no longer hoping for
a badminton game with *les gamins*.

We agreed: if you ask a fellow how
he feels you hurt a fellow's feelings.

The dog ran in diagonals,
macraméing the park. But then

there was the shuttlecock
& the shock of it made the snowy

mouse bite Hazel's ankle & she
kicked a stack of planks which

buried me & only sweetened you.

THE TRANSPARENT HEIR APPARENT

All day the prince's subjects stood under the gold balcony & cheered. They waved when his horse trotted by on its early morning run, just in case he was riding it. He'd been opaque as a child, but his family had a history of similar afflictions—the famous emperor who thought less was more when it came to clothing was a distant relation—so no one was particularly surprised when at age thirteen in the middle of being quizzed on French nouns, the prince's head became see-through & his answer to the question "*Vous voulez . . . ?*" showed a tiny velvet sofa and his French teacher on it with her bodice askew. Every day the prince faded a little more until he shimmered like the barely-there watermarks on palace proclamations. When it was time for him to find a wife, he didn't want someone who would steal the limelight, so he began to comb the country for a bride, who if not transparent, could at least be termed translucent. He was partial to girls whose veins showed through; chose one whose blood branched blue at her temples, whose skin was impossibly pale. One night, watching his queen-to-be sleeping, her vague shape among the linens like a coach with its edges blurred by snow, the prince had an idea: If, through careful intermarriage, the royal family were to become completely invisible, couldn't they replace the gods?

CAN WE SEE

What I thought was
the wind was a bicycle & lo

my head was halved again.
Red buds measled the ground.

Jealous Narcissus bit the river.
The sky was a memoir of blue.

In between the blades of grass hosanna
there was much greener grass.

INTRODUCTION TO THE END

The lovely green
of the preview screen.

1348: Plague   (simple as flypaper)

Introducing the wheeled-out thing,
once wet-lipped on a ledge.   Spare me
                                     your theatrics.
Saw yourself
in half, then.
Make the soufflé fall.

You see—
where you stood, you stand.

When he sees the second train coming
towards you, the hero will save himself.

                                     & you don't want us
                                     to call you
Anything.

                                     Spare me. Please.

INTRODUCTION TO DISEASE

Call me Responsible.

                          (Like all of them
                          it loves an exam.)

Pleased to meetcha.
A charming living space.

                          Thank you.
                          All original, naturally.

Tongue?   Not telling.
(Funny little factory.)

                          I know my diagnosis.
                          Friendlier than the world.
                          Friendlier than the world.

Well do yourself a favor
they say &

                          I do not think we meant it
                          like that.

I do. Like that.

THAT WAS THE FIRST DAY & WE NEVER FORGOT IT

Our questions started small: why was the radio warm when we came home, why did the soufflé fall not once but thrice? At noon the sun shone as per usual, but there were moon-glints on the garbage lids. On the subway train rain began to fall among the silver poles & onto our heads—we didn't see the man in the corner clutching a rosebush, couldn't know that its roots were remembering. That was the first day & we never forgot it, never forgot anything ever again. Within minutes the minimalists had all gone mad. Graffiti artists grumbled, carried whitewash with them. The neighbor's obstinate child checkers my lawn with small white squares—Polaroids she's taken & hurled over the hedge. The cardinals hop backwards from boxwood to boxwood. Today I ducked under the tent-flap of an abandoned bigtop & watched elephants swell from their tracks in the sawdust. I remembered the acrobats & they remembered their nets. But what of the tightrope walker tiptoeing to the supermarket, the clown who can't seem to get his face clean? Sweet one not beside me holding last year's cotton candy, the past is sticking fast. The beaches are sprouting fossil upon fossil & last night at the opera, the spotlight wouldn't stay still. These are the rules I adhere to—one painting per museum, dinner one day, dessert the next. I wish I could see just you.

TOWN OF THEN

I meant me in the general sense
when I said did you want me.

The Old World smoked in the fireplace.
Rain fell in a post-Romantic way.

In a spoon a ceiling fan whirled.
Heads in the planets, toes tucked

under carpets, that's how we got our bodies
through. The drink we drank was cordial.

The amnesiac made a delicious sauce
& traced its radius to remember;

the translator made the sign for horses
backing away from a lump of sugar.

The sun was almost eye-level.
The trains twitched in their tracks.

A RUFFLE, A RENDEZVOUS

Goggles against the windowpane.
Playing chess in gingham.

Split-second snow chandelier.
Underwater constellation of scallops.

A skate frills along the ocean floor—
I don't think it's what I'm looking for.

Equestrian galloping through the rain,
glorious movie-set moon, it isn't

chance if you're waiting for it.

ABANDONED CONVERSATION WITH THE SENSES

In the back they are collecting
bullets so do you really want to talk

about love? When a bee is on my chin
should I not mind it? Shall I let

the pretty water sink the boat?
Learn something from me for once

will you. A tent inside the barn
may be just what we need.

The bull shakes the snow off its back.
Yes its meat is nice to eat.

No it's not a snowstorm.
All this explaining exhausts me.

I'll be leaving some traps in the forest.
Do come admire the trees.

REVERSE SPACE INVADERS

The living fence faltered.
It does make one feel a bit

"other" admitted Sartre.
In the hedges these sentences

were found: Many people derive
satisfaction from things

lemony. In addition,
many people use calculators.

Silly me, said the nugatory
I—I thought I might swim

in our nation's ocean.
Our attackers were silky & small.

Above us, an expository sky.
Grey, then rain, then closing.

LIMELIGHT MEMORANDUM

Machines are no longer
slowly combing the red earth.

There is no one left to explain
the cones in my eyes to me.

I have been given my sentence
& it is not a long one

though it does include the word
quintessential which pleases me.

Accordingly, I am no relation
to the sky but to the mechanical

dragon wrapped in tissue paper
with plastic flames poking

through. I never told you
that if I were born a suitcase

I would want a trailer
with red curtains so I could

pretend to be a lion. But being
matter-of-fact is like a meatpie in

the pocket. It is the way to go.

GOING OFF THE DEEP END INTO CONFECTIONERY

We're the anemones guarding
the gates of infinity,

the boats squidding in the bay.
In the flooded fish market,

dead fish, live fish—who took you
to the Tuileries for a rose-

scented swim? Turn the world
& the page is pink.

Frond-fond & pond-proud,
we sugar the obstacle dark.

EVERYTHING MUST GO

Today's class 3-Deifying:
Godgrass, Godtrees, Godroad.

A sheet of geese bisects the rainstorm.
The water tower is ten storms full.

We practice drawing cubes—
that's the house squared away

& the incubator with Baby.
The dead are in their grid.

O the sleeping bag contains
the body but not the dreaming head.

ACKNOWLEDGMENTS

Thank you to the editors of the following journals for giving a home to these poems:

88: "Shiver & You Have Weather"

American Letters & Commentary: "Address to an Absent Flea," "Limelight Memorandum"

American Poetry Review: "Toe the Line with Me"

Canary River Review: "Poem Including the Seven Deadly Sins"

Columbia: "Meat Ravioli vs. Spaghetti Bolognese"

Conduit: "Our Square of Lawn," "That Was the First Day & We Never Forgot It"

Delmar: "Abandoned Conversation with the Senses," "First Person Fabulous"

Denver Quarterly: "Once upon a Time: A Genre Fable"

Doubletake: "O the Zoetrope & the Periscope Should Be Friends"

Electronic Poetry Review: "Introduction to a Diction," "Introduction to Addiction," "Snowglobe Hypothesis"

Forklift: "If You Like Sugar I'll Like Sugar Too," "Introduction to Narrative"

Good foot: "Reverse Space Invaders," "Shiver & You Have Weather"

Gulf Coast: "Ideas Go Only So Far," "Not So Much Miniature As Far Away"

Indiana Review: "Town of Then"

Insurance: "Baked Alaska, a Theory Of"

La Petite Zine: "Poem Including the Seven Wonders of the Ancient World," "You're Miss Reading"

NC2: "A Ruffle, a Rendezvous," "The Crying Fields"

The New Republic: "Life-Size Is What We Are (A New History of Photography)"

The New Yorker: "Everything Must Go"

The New York Times Book Review: "Diagram of Pretty Please"

Octopus: "Reverberations in the Snail World," "Color by Number," "Bird Transfer"

Open City: "Sergio Valente, Sergio Valente, How You Look Tells the World How You Feel," "To Zanzibar by Motorcar"

Pierogi Press: "This Is Not a Glass Door," "No More Frisson Please"

Ploughshares: "The Crowds Cheered As Gloom Galloped Away," "Introduction to Eden," "Introduction to Disease"

Post Road: "Definition of Weather," "The Difference Between the Need for Consistency & the State of Expectation"

Publishing Online: "Introduction to Circumference," "Introduction to the Swanhouse"

Slope: "Trouble in the Dyad," "Equation with Flowers"

Spork: "Save the Originals"

Swerve: "Going Off the Deep End into Confectionery," "Machine for Jean Rhys," "Can We See," "Introduction to the End," "The Transparent Heir Apparent"

Verse: "Introduction to the World," "Grand Narrative with Chandelier," "Sad Little Breathing Machine"

THANKS

Thank you to my family & friends for everything.

"Bird Transfer" is for Brett Lauer.
"To Zanzibar by Motorcar" is for Mimi Schultz.
"Equation with Flowers" is for Celia Harvey.
"Color by Number" is for Anna Rabinowitz.
"Trouble in the Dyad" is for Alex Garcia Mansilla.
"Abandoned Conversation with the Senses" is for Ellen Harvey.

& thank you for the following title gifts: Lucy Raven for "Not So Much Miniature As Far Away," Lorin Stein and Sergio Valente for "Sergio Valente, Sergio Valente, How You Look Tells the World How You Feel," Clement Greenberg for "Going Off the Deep End into Confectionery," & Rebecca Horn for "The Unconsciousness of Feelings."

MATTHEA HARVEY is the author of *Modern Life, Sad Little Breathing Machine, Pity the Bathtub Its Forced Embrace of the Human Form,* and a children's book, *The Little General and the Giant Snowflake.* Harvey is a contributing editor to *jubilat* and *BOMB.* She teaches poetry at Sarah Lawrence College and lives in Brooklyn.

The text of this book has been set in Adobe Garamond, drawn by Robert Slimbach and based on type cut by Claude Garamond in the sixteenth century. Book design by Wendy Holdman. Composition by Stanton Publication Services, Inc., St. Paul, Minnesota. Manufactured by Thomson-Shore on acid-free paper.